Primary Sources in World History

# THE INDUSTRIAL REVOLUTION

**ENZO GEORGE**

Cavendish Square

New York

Published in 2017 by Cavendish Square Publishing, LLC
243 5th Avenue, Suite 136 New York, NY 10016

© 2017 Brown Bear Books Ltd

Website: cavendishsq.com

CPSIA compliance information: Batch #CS16CSQ.

All websites were available and accurate when this book went to press.

Library of Congress Cataloging-in-Publication Data

Names: George, Enzo.
Title: The Industrial Revolution / Enzo George.
Description: New York : Cavendish Square, 2017. | Series: Primary sources in world history | Includes index.
Identifiers: ISBN 9781502618177 (library bound) | ISBN 9781502620187 (ebook)
Subjects: LCSH: Industrial revolution—Juvenile literature. | Economic history—Juvenile literature.
Classification: LCC HC51.G46 2017 | DDC 909.81—dc23

For Brown Bear Books Ltd:
Editorial Director: Lindsey Lowe
Managing Editor: Tim Cooke
Children's Publisher: Anne O'Daly
Design Manager: Keith Davis
Designer: Lynne Lennon
Picture Manager: Sophie Mortimer

Picture Credits:
Front Cover: Getty Images: Liszt Collection/Heritage Images main; Shutterstock: ilolab map.
Interior: C.F. Cheffins: John Snow 35; Hedley Fitton: History of Runcorn 8; Google Earth: Justin C 34; Stephen C. Dickson: 24; International Institute of Social History, nl: 33; Library of Congress: 25, 30, 38, 40, 42, 43; Robert Hunt Library: 13, 28, 41, London in Miniature 22; Shutterstock: Everett Historical 31, 32, Marzolino 39; Thinkstock: istockphoto 15, 18, Elena Perez/istockphoto 9, Ian Woolcock/istockphoto 6, Photos.com 7, 10, 12, 14, 16, 20, 21, 26, 29, 36, 37; Topfoto: 17, World History Archive 19; V&A: 23; Wellcome Images: 27.

Brown Bear Books has made every attempt to contact the copyright holder.
If you have any information please contact licensing@brownbearbooks.co.uk

We believe the extracts included in this book to be material in the public domain.
Anyone having further information should contact licensing@brownbearbooks.co.uk

Printed in the United States of America

# CONTENTS

# INTRODUCTION

**Primary sources are the best way to get close to people from the past. They include the things people wrote in diaries, letters, or books; the paintings, drawings, maps, or cartoons they created; and even the buildings they constructed, the clothes they wore, or the objects they owned. Such sources often reveal a lot about how people saw themselves and how they thought about their world.**

This book collects a range of primary sources from the Industrial Revolution. The period is only vaguely defined. Most historians agree that it began in the early 1700s and continued until the late 1800s.

The Industrial Revolution was a period of technological innovation and social change. Many developments were led by Britain, which also experienced the worst problems associated with the growth of industry. The invention of the steam engine led to the concentration of manufacturing in large factories. In turn, this led to the growth of industrial towns as people moved from the countryside in order to find work. For most workers life was hard and miserable. Meanwhile, improvements in transportation such as the steam locomotive and steamship made it possible for people, goods, and ideas to travel farther and faster. Britain relied on its overseas empire to provide raw materials for its industries and markets for its products.

# HOW TO USE THIS BOOK

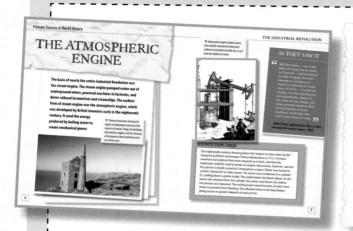

Each spread contains at least one primary source. Look out for "Source Explored" boxes that explain images from the Industrial Revolution and who made them and why. There are also "As They Saw It" boxes that contain quotes from people of the period.

Some boxes contain more detailed information about a particular aspect of a subject. The subjects are arranged in roughly chronological order. They focus on key events or people. There is a full timeline of the period at the back of the book.

Some spreads feature a longer extract from a contemporary eyewitness. Look for the colored introduction that explains who the writer is and the origin of his or her account. These accounts are often accompanied by a related visual primary source.

# THE ATMOSPHERIC ENGINE

The basis of nearly the entire Industrial Revolution was the steam engine. The steam engine pumped water out of underground mines, powered machines in factories, and drove railroad locomotives and steamships. The earliest form of steam engine was the atmospheric engine, which was developed by British inventors early in the eighteenth century. It used the energy produced by boiling water to create mechanical power.

▼ *Thomas Newcomen invented his engine to help pump water out of tin mines in Cornwall. Today, the buildings that held the engines and the chimneys of the furnaces that heated the water can still be seen.*

▼ *Newcomen's engine rocked a beam that could be attached to chains and pulleys to raise loads of water, tin, or soil from the depths of a mine.*

66 Mr Newcomen ... was in the habit of visiting the tin mines in Cornwall ... and had derived his title of captain from his attempts to introduce his engine for draining the mines, many of which ... worked out so deep, as to be unproductive and unprofitable, merely for the want of some cheaper and more powerful machines than the hand-pumps or horse-machines, which they then used to drain them of water. 99

—John Farey explains how Newcomen invented the steam engine, 1827.

## SOURCE EXPLORED

This eighteenth-century drawing shows the "engine to raise water by fire" designed by British ironmonger Thomas Newcomen in 1712. Previous inventors had realized that water expands as it boils, and that this expansion could be used to power an engine. Newcomen, however, was the first person to build a practical "atmospheric engine." Water was heated in a boiler (labeled B) to make steam. The steam was condensed in a cylinder (C), pulling down a piston inside. This pulled down the beam above. As the steam was released from the cylinder, the piston and beam rose before the process was repeated. The rocking beam raised buckets of water from mines to prevent them flooding. This allowed mines to be dug deeper, giving access to greater deposits of coal and tin.

# THE FIRST CANAL

▲ *This drawing from the 1880s shows barges on the Bridgewater Canal alongside a soapworks in Runcorn.*

The early Industrial Revolution depended on water for transportation. The French had pioneered canal building in Europe, but the first industrial canal opened in Britain on July 17, 1761. It was named the Bridgewater Canal for its builder, the Duke of Bridgewater, who wanted it to transport coal from his mines to power the growing number of factories in Manchester. The 39-mile-long (65 kilometer) canal dramatically reduced the cost of transporting coal into the city.

▲ Barges were towed along the Canal du Midi by horses on the towpath that ran alongside the length of the waterway.

### SOURCE EXPLORED

The Duke of Bridgewater was inspired to build his canal after a visit to southern France, where he was impressed by the Canal du Midi in Languedoc. The French had begun building the 150-mile (240 km) long canal in 1666 in order to transport wheat between the Mediterranean Sea and the Atlantic Ocean. The canal in France included 328 different structures, including aqueducts, tunnels, bridges, and locks. Bridgewater planned his own canal so that it followed the contours of the land, reducing the need for expensive locks to raise boats between different levels.

The author Samuel Smiles was an enthusiastic supporter of the Industrial Revolution. Here he describes how the Bridgewater Canal connected to the coal mines in around 1861:

“ It is at Worsley basin that the canal enters the bottom of the hill by a subterranean channel which extends to a great distance—connecting the different workings of the mine—so that the coals can be readily transported in boats to their place of sale ... In Brindley's time this subterranean canal, hewn out of the rock, was only about a mile in length, but now extends to nearly 40 miles [64 km] underground in all directions. When the tunnel passed through earth or coal, the arching was of brickwork, but where it passed through rock, it was simply hewn out. This tunnel acts not only as a drain and water-feeder for the canal itself, but as a means of carrying the facilities of the navigation [canal] through the very heart of the collieries. ”

# FIRST FACTORIES

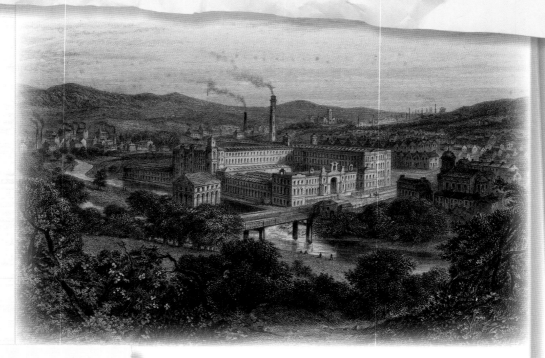

▲ Salts Mill opened on the Aire River near Bradford in 1853. Its 1,200 looms produced 18 miles (29 km) of cotton every day.

Among the first industries to be transformed by mechanization were the cotton and woollen industries. Previously, rural families had spun yarn and woven cloth by hand in their own homes. Now steam engines increased the speed of production by powering spinning machines and looms. Such machines were too large for homes, so they were set up in purpose-built factories and mills. The impact on British society was huge. Cottage industries died out and increasing numbers of people moved to work in the growing towns and cities.

◄ *This engraving from about 1880 shows a female factory worker operating a spinning jenny. She turns the large wheel by hand to wind yarn onto a number of spindles at the same time.*

## SOURCE EXPLORED

This drawing shows a female worker looking after a machine known as a spinning jenny. Invented by James Hargreaves in 1764. It mechanized the work of hand spinners, who spun strands of cotton into thread. Hargreaves' machine allowed a single worker to produce eight spools of thread at the same time. As Hargreaves improved the machine, that number rose to one-hundred-and-twenty spools. In 1769, Richard Arkwright patented a spinning frame powered by water, and in 1779 Samuel Crompton combined the two inventions to create the spinning mule. It revolutionized the production of cotton. Now up to 1,320 spindles of cotton and other fibers could be spun together at the same time, leading to a huge expansion in the production of textiles.

## COTTONOPOLIS

The production of cotton transformed Manchester in northwest England from being a small market town in the early eighteenth century to becoming the most important city of the Industrial Revolution. Its population grew from 10,000 in 1720 to 70,000 in 1800 and 140,000 by 1830. The city was home to the first water-powered textile mill in the world, opened by Richard Arkwright in 1781. More mills followed, together with vast warehouses in the downtown area to store raw cotton and finished cloth. By 1871, Manchester and its neighboring towns produced about a third of the world's cotton. The city earned the nickname Cottonopolis.

# COTTON PRODUCTION

▲ *This engraving from 1869 is entitled* The First Cotton Gin. *It shows slaves processing cotton with a gin some seventy years earlier.*

As more textile mills appeared in Britain, demand increased for cotton to make yarn. Cotton fiber came from the United States and also from Britain's empire. Ships brought US cotton to ports such as Liverpool, which also exported finished cotton goods throughout the empire. Producing cotton was slow work, however, until Eli Whitney invented the cotton gin in 1794. The new machine speeded up the rate of production. By 1860, the US South supplied about 80 percent of Britain's raw cotton.

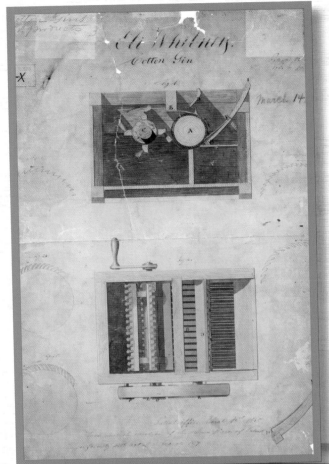

## SOURCES OF COTTON

The demand for cotton grew in Britain in the seventeenth century. Most cotton was originally imported from Britain's colony in India, but by the 1840s industrialization meant India could no longer produce as much cotton as British factories required. Instead, British industrialists looked to the United States. Demand encouraged planters in the South to produce more cotton, which required more slaves. The number of slave states grew from six in 1790 to fifteen in 1860. By encouraging the spread of slavery, some historians believe the cotton gin contributed to the eventual outbreak of the Civil War in 1861.

◄ *Whitney's design for the cotton gin (short for "engine") was so widely copied that his firm went bust in 1797.*

## SOURCE EXPLORED

This illustration accompanied Eli Whitney's application for a patent for his cotton gin in 1794. Other models of cotton gin had been used before, but Whitney's was the first machine to be widely used. It comprised a box containing a roller stuck with fine hooks. As a handle was turned, the hooks pulled the fibers through a mesh, separating them from the seeds, which would not fit through. The seeds were removed and planted, while the fibers were used to spin into yarn. The cotton gin made growing cotton far more profitable. New plantations were set up throughout the South. Growing and harvesting cotton still had to be done by hand, however, so the number of slaves in the South increased.

# FACTORY LIFE

In the early 1800s, workers in the new factories endured difficult conditions. Factories had appeared so quickly that there were few rules to protect the people who worked there. Long hours were spent standing at dangerous, unfenced machines and workers had only short breaks. Children as young as four or five did jobs for which adults were too big, such as crawling under machines to mend broken threads. It was not until 1833 that the British government introduced the Factory Act to try to improve working conditions.

▼ This engraving from 1851 shows women grinding pen nibs in a mechanized factory in Birmingham in Britain. Giant drive belts turn the grinding wheels.

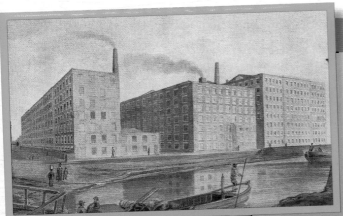

▲ *In Manchester and elsewhere, mills tended to be clustered. They needed water for transportation and to power their machines.*

## SOURCE EXPLORED

This drawing shows the Sedgwick Mill in Ancoats, Manchester, in around 1820. As cotton and wool production became more mechanized, machines grew bigger. They had to be housed in vast purpose-built buildings, which, in turn, needed to be next to rivers or canals so that the raw materials and finished products could easily be transported. The factories had large windows to let in natural light. Ancoats was planned as a new industrial area of Manchester to house factories full of steam-powered machinery.

In his account of working as a boy in a Scottish factory, James Myles compares daily life for a child factory worker in 1827 with that of a slave in Carolina:

" The lash of the slave driver was never more unsparingly used in Carolina on the unfortunate slaves than the canes and 'whangs' of mill foremen were then used on helpless factory boys. When I went to a spinning mill I was about seven years of age. I had to get out of bed every morning at five o'clock, commence work at halfpast five, drop at nine for breakfast, begin again at halfpast nine, work until two, which was the dinner hour, start again at halfpast two, and continue until halfpast seven at night. Such were the nominal hours; but in reality there were no regular hours, masters and managers did with us as they liked. The clocks at the factories were often put forward in the morning and back at night, and instead of being instruments for the measurement of time, they were used as cloaks for cheatery and oppression. "

# AN IDEAL FACTORY

▲ *This colored engraving shows New Lanark in about 1815. The complex included four cotton mills together with row houses and tenements for the workers.*

On January 1, 1800, Robert Owen took over the running of his father-in-law's textile mills in New Lanark, Scotland. Owen belonged to a new type of so-called "enlightened" factory owner, in contrast to those who only wanted to maximize their profits by exploiting workers as much as possible. Owens had revolutionary ideas: he believed that keeping his workers happy would make them work harder. He introduced many radical measures, including a village of houses for his workers with a school to educate their children and a village shop with prices his workers could afford.

Robert Southey was an English poet who visited Owen's mills in 1819 on a trip around Scotland. He described New Lanark as being a modern utopia, which means a place where everything is perfect:

" It is needless to say anything more of the Mills than they are perfect of their kind, according to the present state of mechanical science, and that they appeared to be under admirable management; they are thoroughly clean, and so carefully ventilated, that there was no unpleasant smell in any of the apartments. Everything required for the machinery is made upon the spot.... There are stores also from which people are supplied with all the necessaries of life. They have a credit there ... but many deal elsewhere if they choose.... A large building is just completed, with ball and concert and lecture rooms, all for 'the formation of character'... "

## SOURCE EXPLORED

This twentieth-century photograph shows workers' cottages built by Robert Owen in New Lanark. Owen not only provided housing. He banned children under ten from working and set up schools instead, including the first elementary school in the world. Owen did not believe in physical punishment, which was common in other factories. Instead, he used "silent monitors." These colored blocks hung next to each machine displaying colors, from white for excellent work to black for bad work. Owen believed the monitor encouraged workers without the need for violence.

▲ Providing good housing for workers was a key part of what Robert Owen called his "Great Experiment," together with educational and workplace reform.

# TREVITHICK'S LOCOMOTIVE

Born in 1771, Richard Trevithick was an engineer and inventor from Cornwall, England. He developed the first small, light high-pressure steam engines that could be used to raise tin, water, and waste more efficiently from local tin mines. In the early 1800s, he turned his attention to developing the world's first working steam locomotive. He successfully experimented with miniature steam engines before designing a full-size model. On February 21, 1804, Trevithick's steam locomotive pulled a train 10 miles (16 km) along a tramway at Pen-y-darren ironworks in South Wales.

◀ This portrait of Richard Trevithick in front of a wild-looking landscape was painted in 1816 by the artist John Linnell. Trevithick solved many of the problems of converting a stationery steam engine into a moving locomotive.

*◀ Trevithick built a circular track in central London to show that rail travel was quicker than traveling by horse. However, an unenthusiastic public response caused him to give up building locomotives.*

## SOURCE EXPLORED

This contemporary drawing by the artist Thomas Rowlandson shows Trevithick's locomotive *Catch-me-who-can* in London in 1808. Although it had reached speeds of 5 miles per hour (8 kilometers per hour), the Pen-y-darren locomotive had proved impractical because its weight broke the cast-iron rails on which it ran. Despite this setback, Trevithick designed a new engine, the *Catch-me-who-can*. He constructed a circular track in London and charged passengers for riding in a carriage behind the locomotive. It reached speeds of 12 miles per hour (19 kmh), but like the Pen-y-darren locomotive it broke the rails. Trevithick abandoned his experiment without ever proving that the steam locomotive had a practical use.

## JAMES WATT

Trevithick's locomotive was made possible in part by improvements made to the atmospheric steam engine by the Scottish engineer James Watt in the 1760s. Watt realized that early steam engines were inefficient because the piston chamber constantly cooled and reheated as steam expanded and was condensed. Watt designed a more efficient engine in which the steam was condensed in a separate chamber. He also designed a gear that turned the up-and-down motion of the piston into a rotary, or turning, motion. This allowed the steam engine to be used for tasks such as milling or weaving. It also opened the way for the eventual design of a moving steam locomotive.

# THE *ROCKET*

In 1821, the British engineer George Stephenson was commissioned to build a railroad between Stockton and Darlington. He made the rails from wrought iron rather than cast iron to avoid them being crushed by heavy locomotives. Later that decade, Stephenson built the Liverpool and Manchester Railway. He used embankments and cuttings to keep the route as flat as possible to avoid strain on the engines. In 1829, Stephenson's locomotive *Rocket* won trials to run on the new line. It was lighter and more efficient than any previous locomotive, with a top speed of 28 miles per hour (45 kmh). Stephenson's innovations earned him the nickname of "the Father of the Railway."

▼ This 1831 illustration shows first-class (top) and second-class passenger trains on the Liverpool and Manchester Railway.

◀ *The first train on the Stockton and Darlington Railway had thirty-six wagons. It traveled at an average of only 4 miles per hour (6.4 kmh).*

## SOURCE EXPLORED

This drawing shows Stephenson's *Locomotion No. 1* pulling passenger cars at the opening of the Stockton and Darlington Railway on September 27, 1825. By the time he designed *Rocket* four years later, Stephenson used wooden wheels for lightness and a separate tender, or water tank. These made the locomotive lighter and faster than earlier models. Some contemporary observers predicted that passengers might suffocate. They feared that traveling at high speeds would create a vacuum with no air to breathe. This proved inaccurate, but *Rocket*'s debut was marred by an accident. A politician in the official opening party was knocked down by *Rocket*. He became the first person to be killed by a train.

## AS THEY SAW IT

" You can't imagine how strange it seemed to be journeying on thus, without any visible cause of progress other than the magical machine, with its flying white breath and rhythmical, unvarying pace, between these rocky walls ... Bridges were thrown from side to side across the top of these cliffs, and the people looking down upon us from them seemed like pigmies standing in the sky. "

—Writer Fanny Kemble describes a trial journey on the *Rocket* in a letter of August 26, 1830.

# CHARLES DICKENS

Charles Dickens published fifteen novels between 1836 and 1870, and established himself as the greatest novelist of the Industrial Revolution. He was brought up in poverty. His father was imprisoned for being in debt and as a child Dickens was sent to work making shoe polish. He only attended school briefly but went on to become a newspaper reporter and novelist. Dickens was committed to social reform. Works such as *Oliver Twist* and *Hard Times* described in detail the difficult lives of the poor and vulnerable in cities such as London.

◄ A gang of boys pick the pocket of a gentleman in this illustration from the 1837–1839 novel Oliver Twist. The book tells the story of an orphan, Oliver, who becomes part of a street gang in London.

Dickens published *Hard Times* in 1854. His fictional setting was "Coketown," which symbolizes the lack of compassion the factory owners have for their workers:

> " Coketown ... was a town of red brick, or of brick that would have been red if smoke and ashes had allowed it; but as matters stood it was a town of unnatural red and black like the painted face of a savage. It was a town of machinery and tall chimneys, out of which interminable serpents of smoke trailed themselves for ever and ever, and never got uncoiled. It had a black canal in it, and a river that ran purple with ill-smelling dye, and vast piles of building full of windows where there was a rattling and a trembling all day long, and where the piston of the steam-engine worked monotonously up and down, like the head of an elephant in a state of melancholy madness. "

## SOURCE EXPLORED

Most of Dickens's novels were based in and around London. Parts of the capital were particularly poor and crowded. This 1872 engraving by the French artist Gustave Doré shows the Seven Dials neighborhood of Covent Garden. First laid out in the 1690s, by the mid-nineteenth century Seven Dials had become an overcrowded, miserable slum for the city's poorest residents. It had a reputation for crime and violence. For many Londoners it was too dangerous even to visit.

▼ *Doré's wood engraving shows Dudley Street, known as the "worst slum" in London.*

# THE GREAT STEAMSHIPS

In 1833 the engineer Isambard Kingdom Brunel was hired by the Great Western Railway (GWR) to construct a railroad from London to Bristol. In 1835, Brunel proposed to GWR that they build a steamship to provide regular crossings of the Atlantic to North America. His critics believed steamships needed too much fuel to make long voyages, but Brunel designed the paddlesteamer SS *Great Western*, which first sailed to New York in 1838. The ship made the crossing in less than sixteen days with fuel to spare.

◀ On November 3, 1857, Brunel attempted to launch another steamship, the SS Great Eastern. *Brunel is in the center, with his assistant Henry Wakefield (left) and the politician Lord Derby. The launch failed and took place the following January.*

◀ *The* Great Eastern *was so large it had five funnels to release the smoke from the fires that drove its steam engines.*

## SOURCE EXPLORED

This print is based on a painting created by Edwin Weedon in 1858. It shows Brunel's steamship *Great Eastern*, which that year began to carry passengers and mail to Britain's colonies in India and Australia. Like the *Great Western*, it had both paddlewheels and masts. However, Brunel had also built the first propeller-driven steamship in 1843, the SS *Great Britain*, and the *Great Eastern* also had a propeller. Six times bigger than any other ship, the *Great Eastern* was the largest vessel afloat until the late nineteenth century. It was an economic failure, however, because it never filled its four thousand passenger beds, and was later used only for cargo. Despite its failure, the ship set a precedent for the larger ocean liners that followed.

## A GREAT ENGINEER

Isambard Kingdom Brunel is one of the greatest engineers in history. The transatlantic steamships were perhaps his greatest achievements. Earlier engineers had got the math wrong. They believed such a ship would have to carry so much coal to fuel its engines that there would be no room left for cargo or passengers. Brunel worked out that in fact the coal required did not increase dramatically with the ship's size. Brunel was burned in an accident during trials of the Great Eastern. He died from a stroke shortly after its maiden voyage.

# THE TELEGRAPH

By the 1830s communications were still limited to the speed at which a messenger or a written message could travel by horse or boat. That changed with the invention of the telegraph. The US inventor Samuel B. Morse claimed to be the first to envisage conveying messages by sending electric pulses along a wire in 1832. He first demonstrated his system in 1838. Two British inventors claimed to have invented a similar system at the same time, but Morse's system proved cheaper. It was adopted in North America and around the world. By 1861, telegraph wires had been erected across the whole North American continent, joining the West and East Coasts.

▼ A Pony Express rider greets a man erecting telelgraph wires in the American West in 1861. The telegraph put the Pony Express message-delivery service out of business.

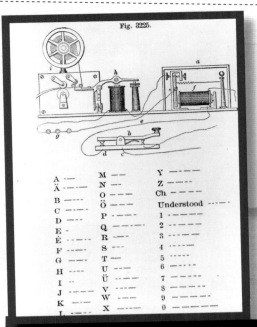

◀ *The code Samuel Morse devised for the telegraph was named for him. It used patterns of long and short pulses to represent individual letters and numbers. Today the code is usually written as a series of dashes and dots.*

## TAMING THE WEST

One of the most significant impacts of the telegraph came in the development of the American West. Throughout the mid-nineteenth century, settlers headed west to the Great Plains and beyond, to the West Coast. At the time, these territories lay beyond effective government control. Overland communications between the central government and the West took days or weeks. Lacking organized law and order, the region gained a reputation as the "Wild West." The coming of the telegraph helped change the situation. Now lawmakers in Washington, DC, could communicate rapidly with civil servants in the West, while they could also receive rapid news of events in even the farthest parts of the country.

## SOURCE EXPLORED

This diagram appeared in a US mechanical dictionary in 1877. It shows Samuel Morse's apparatus for sending and receiving telegraph signals. It also shows the code of long and short signals Samuel Morse devised for letters and numbers. An operator used a key to tap out signals at one end of the wire. The operator at the other end translated the signals back into letters. Morse was best known as a portrait painter but in 1832 he had the idea of sending messages long distances over a wire using electrical pulses. He first demonstrated the telegraph in January 1838, and the first line opened between Baltimore and Washington, DC, on May 24, 1844. The first message sent by telegraph was a quote from the Bible: "What hath God wrought." The first transcontinental telegraph was completed in 1861.

# THE BIRTH OF COMMUNISM

▲ *This photograph of Karl Marx was taken in 1875. Marx was expelled from his homeland of Prussia for his political ideas and spent much of his life in Britain.*

By the mid-nineteenth century, industrialization had changed the shape of European society. The power of the traditional nobility had been weakened. The factory owners belonged to a growing middle class, or bourgeoisie. Unskilled workers, meanwhile, labored for poor wages and little satisfaction. In the 1840s a new political ideology, communism, emerged. It argued that the workers, or proletariat, should revolt in order to create a classless society in which their contribution was more valued.

## SOURCE EXPLORED

This is a page from the original German manuscript of *The Communist Manifesto*. The pamphlet summarized the political beliefs of the German socialist and philosopher Karl Marx. Marx wrote *The Manifesto* with his friend Friedrich Engels in 1848, while they were both living in London. The work sets out their belief that industrial society suffered from great inequalities of wealth and political influence. These inequalities would lead workers to rise up in order to create a communist society in which everyone was more equal. Only a violent revolution would overthrow the old order. The book's publication in 1848 coincided with revolutions in many European cities, including Berlin and Paris. The possibility of a communist revolution seemed very real.

▲ *Only one page survives of the first draft of* The Communist Manifesto. *It is in Marx's handwriting apart from two lines at the top of the page later added by his wife, Jenny von Westphalen.*

## AS THEY SAW IT

❝ The Communists everywhere support every revolutionary movement against the existing social and political order of things.... Their ends can be attained only by the forcible overthrow of all existing social conditions. Let the ruling classes tremble at a Communistic revolution. The proletarians have nothing to lose but their chains. They have a world to win. Working Men of All Countries, Unite! ❞

—Karl Marx in *The Communist Manifesto*, 1848.

# PIONEERING PHYSICIAN

As industrial cities grew more crowded, the poor lived in terrible conditions. Homes were cramped and lacked even basic sanitation. In such overcrowded, dirty conditions, disease was common and often fatal. In 1854 a cholera outbreak caused many deaths in Soho in London. The physician John Snow puzzled about its cause. He questioned the contemporary belief that the disease was carried in the air.

◀ The pump at the heart of the cholera outbreak is preserved as a memorial in Broad Street, London. The nearby pub is named the John Snow for the famous physician.

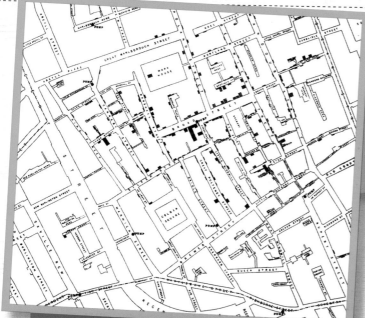

◀ Snow's map of cholera deaths and public water pumps created a whole new field of using maps to study the spread of diseases.

## SOURCE EXPLORED

This map of Soho was created by John Snow in 1854 to map the cases of cholera. Each black mark indicates a death caused by the disease. The map revealed that most deaths were concentrated around a pump in Broad Street. Before many homes had running water, pumps provided water for households. As Snow investigated, he heard about people who had died after drinking water from the pump, while neighbors who used other pumps remained free of the disease. Examination of the Broad Street pump showed that the water had been contaminated by a baby's dirty diaper. The handle was removed from the pump and the cholera outbreak ended. Snow had not only shown that cholera was a waterborne rather than an airborne disease. He had also founded the science of epidemiology, the study of how diseases are spread.

## LEADING DOCTOR

John Snow was one of the most important physicians to have lived. His discovery that cholera was transmitted by dirty water led directly to London improving its sewerage and water systems to eliminate the disease. It also led to the creation of the study of epidemiology and to the founding of the public health system and preventative medicine. Snow was also one of the earliest users of anesthetics during surgery. He administered chloroform as an anesthetic to Queen Victoria during the births of her last two children in 1853 and 1857.

# THE INDIAN MUTINY

▲ *This colored engraving from about 1860 shows the death of the British brigadier Adrian Hope during a clash with Indian troops at the fort of Roodamow in April 1858.*

By the 1820s, India was a vital marketplace for Britain's industrial output. Britain's East India Company dominated all aspects of life in India. Supported by its own army, the trading company built roads, railroads, and schools. It also set up a bureaucracy to govern India. Many Indians resented British attempts to interfere with their traditional ways of life, however. In 1857, Indian soldiers in the British-controlled Indian Army began a two-year mutiny against their masters that would have a major impact on the future of India.

## SOURCE EXPLORED

This nineteenth-century drawing shows sepoys, or infantrymen in Britain's Indian Army. The Indian Mutiny began in 1857 when sepoys in the city of Meerut rose against their British officers. They had heard a rumor that the cartridges for a new rifle were greased with pig and cow fat. The cartridges had to be bitten open, but Hindus and Muslims were forbidden to eat pork or beef, respectively, and the Indian soldiers were outraged. The mutiny spread to other cities, including the capital, Delhi. Both the British and the Indian troops treated the other with great brutality. The rebellion was put down in 1858, but it did lead to change. The East India Company lost its power. The British Crown took direct control of India, starting the era of the British Raj.

▲ This British drawing shows sepoys during the Indian Mutiny. The men are shown as being scruffy, in contrast to the smartness and order the British associated with their own troops.

## AS THEY SAW IT

" Reports strong that Delhi has fallen. The whole district around Agra is disorganized, we are living as if in a state of siege. Not a letter from any part of the country comes. No news from Calcutta for three weeks.... Yesterday a party of armed Volunteers on horseback went out to Fultiabad to help escort in the ladies who are coming in from Etawah. "

—Maria Amelia Vansittart, wife of a British officer in the Bengal Army, writes in her diary on June 16, 1857.

# THE ABOLITION OF SLAVERY

By the end of the eighteenth century, opposition to slavery was growing. Britain, one of the key countries involved in shipping African slaves across the Atlantic, abolished the slave trade in 1807. It abolished slavery throughout the British Empire in 1833. In the United States, slavery had disappeared from the North. In the South, however, the whole economy depended on slave labor. An abolition movement grew up to call for change.

◀ Politician William Wilberforce led the anti-slavery campaign in Britain after becoming an Evangelical Christian in 1785. He died in 1833, just before slavery was abolished in the British Empire.

▼ This commemorative poster shows the text of the Emancipation Proclamation surrounded by scenes of African American slaves enjoying their new freedom.

## AS THEY SAW IT

" I do order and declare that all persons held as slaves within said designated States and parts of States are, and henceforward shall be, free; and that the Executive Government of the United States, including the military and naval authorities thereof, will recognize and maintain the freedom of said persons. "

—Abraham Lincoln, draft of the Emancipation Proclamation, September 22, 1862.

## SOURCE EXPLORED

This print of Abraham Lincoln's Emancipation Proclamation was published in 1864, the year after the Proclamation became law on January 1, 1863. The Civil War was still going on, and the Proclamation declared all slaves in Confederate states free. It effectively abolished slavery in the United States. The war itself was partly caused by Southern fears that Lincoln would abolish slavery after he was elected president in November 1860. Southerners argued that slavery actually benefited slaves, and that Northerners did not understand their "peculiar institution." After Lincoln's election the Southern states quit the Union, beginning the war. When it seemed clear that the North would win, Lincoln took the chance to issue the Emancipation Proclamation.

# RAILROADS IN NORTH AMERICA

The United States soon adopted railroads from Britain. The first US line opened in 1830 from Baltimore to the Ohio River, beginning a construction boom. Railroads helped the North win the Civil War (1861–1865) by allowing it to move men quickly. The first transcontinental railroad was completed in 1869. By 1890 the United States had nearly 130,000 miles (210,000 km) of track.

▼ This poster commemorates the first regular passenger service in North America. The service ran on the Mohawk & Hudson Railroad beginning August 1831. It used an engine from England and carriages modeled on stagecoaches.

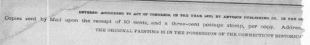

Copies sent by Mail upon the receipt of 10 cents, and a three-cent postage stamp, per copy. Address...

THE ORIGINAL PAINTING IS IN THE POSSESSION OF THE CONNECTICUT HISTORIC...

## The First Steam Railroad Passenger Train in America.

In 1826 a Charter was granted to the MOHAWK & HUDSON R. R. Co. for a Railroad to run from Albany to Schenectady, N. Y.; 16 miles. In 1830 work was commenced on the Road, which went through the populous towns along the open streets, without restriction or fear of the consequences, and travelled across fields, up hill and down. The land was either given to the Railway Company, or sold for a trifling consideration, and it was finished in 1831. Both Locomotive Engines and Horses were used on the Road, and the tickets were sold at stores or shops, or by the conductor, and the trains proceeded at a very slow rate. Stationary Engines were at the top of the hills, and the train was hauled up hill or let down hill by a strong rope. The brakemen used hand-levers to stop or check the train.

The first Steam Railroad Passenger Excursion Train in America was run on this Road in 1831. The Engine was named "JOHN BULL," it was imported from England — its weight was 4 tons. The Engineer was John Hampson, an Englishman. There were fifteen passengers on the Train of two coaches, among whom were the following.—(commencing at the rear of the train.)

| | | | |
|---|---|---|---|
| 1. UNKNOWN. | 6. MAJOR MEGGS, - - - Sheriff. | 12. UNKNOWN. |
| 2. LEWIS BENEDICT. | 7. UNKNOWN. | 13. EX GOV. JOS. C. YATES. |
| 3. JAMES ALEXANDER, - - Pres't Commercial Bank. | 8. BILLY WINNE, - - - Penny Postman. | 14. UNKNOWN. |
| 4. CHARLES E. DUDLEY, - Dudley Observatory. | 9. UNKNOWN. | 15. UNKNOWN. |
| 5. JACOB HAYES, - - - - - High Constable of New York. | 10. UNKNOWN. | 16. JOHN HAMPSON, - - - Engineer. |
| | 11. THURLOW WEED. | |

## SOURCE EXPLORED

This photograph shows the ceremony to mark the completion of the first transcontinental railroad on May 10, 1869. The Central Pacific Railroad from California to the west and the Union Pacific Railroad from Iowa to the east met at Promontory Summit in Utah Territory. The final spike was driven home with a hammer by Leland Stanford of the Central Pacific Railroad and Thomas Durant of the Union Pacific Railroad, watched by a crowd of dignitaries and railroad engineers. Telegraph wires flashed the news across the United States with the single word, "Done." In 1876, the Transcontinental Express crossed the continent from New York City to San Francisco in just 83 hours and 39 minutes.

## AS THEY SAW IT

" The spike was given its first blow by President Stanford and Vice President Durant followed. Neither hit the spike the first time, but hit the rail, and were greeted by the lusty cheers of the onlookers ... Then the two trains were run together ... and the engineers of the two locomotives each broke a bottle of champagne on the other's engine. Then it was declared that the connection was made and the Atlantic and Pacific were joined together never to be parted. "

—General Grenville M. Dodge, chief engineer of the Union Pacific Railroad, Utah, May 10, 1869.

◄ Railroad officials and workers at the Golden Spike Ceremony in Utah.

# CHILD LABOR

▲ *Child labor remained a problem into the twentieth century and beyond. This young female worker was photographed in a cotton mill in South Carolina in 1908.*

Children were a valuable source of labor during the Industrial Revolution. They worked in factories and down coal mines. They could do jobs adults could not, such as getting into tight spaces in order to clean machines. Children could be easily disciplined and they were cheap to employ. In the 1830s and 1840s new laws banned very young children from working in factories and mines and limited the hours that older children were allowed to work. It was not until the 1860s and 1870s that other forms of child labor, such as climbing up chimneys to clean them, were forbidden by the law.

▲ *This drawing shows young sweeps in Paris, France, where they faced similar conditions to those in London.*

## SOURCE EXPLORED

A group of child chimney sweeps play ring-a-ring o'roses in this drawing from 1857. Their fun would be brief, because life for sweeps was hard. Small "climbing boys" were sent up chimneys to clean them. Some girls were also employed. The children were often orphans who were forced to do the work. Some became stuck and suffocated. Others were injured or had their lungs permanently damaged by soot. Concern about their working conditions was raised in the popular 1863 novel by Charles Kingsley, *The Water Babies*. In 1875 a sweep was tried and imprisoned for allowing a climbing boy to die. The case finally led to a law banning child sweeps.

In 1847 the social reformer Samuel Kydd discussed child labor in his book *The History of the Factory Movement*:

" Children of a very tender age are employed, many of them collected from the workhouses in London and Westminster, and transported in crowds as apprentices to masters resident many hundred miles distant.... These children are usually too long confined to work, in close rooms, often during the whole night. The air they breathe from the oil, etc., employed in the machinery, and other circumstances, is injurious [harmful]; little attention is paid to their cleanliness; and frequent changes from a warm and dense to a cold and thin atmosphere are predisposing causes to sickness and debility [weakness], and particularly to the epidemic fever which is so generally to be met with in these factories. "

# THE ELECTRICAL AGE

The late nineteenth century is sometimes known as the Second Industrial Revolution. It saw a series of technological innovations. One of the most important was the spread of a new form of power. In the 1820s, the British scientist Michael Faraday discovered how to generate electricity with magnets. That led to the development of the electric motor. Later inventions that were also based on electricity included the telegraph and telephone, the gramophone, and the radio.

◀ This photograph shows waterfalls illuminated by electric lights at the Louisiana Purchase Exposition in St. Louis in 1904.

◀ Joseph Swan patented the first incandescent lightbulb in 1860. He later successfully took Edison to court for stealing his ideas.

## SOURCE EXPLORED

The British-born scientist Joseph Wilson Swan works in his laboratory in 1910. Swan competed with the American inventor Thomas Edison to invent the lightbulb. Both men understood that light could be generated by using electricity to heat thin strips, or filaments, of a conducting material. Swan invented the first incandescent lightbulb, but in 1879 Edison used a carbon filament to create the first lightbulb that lasted long enough to have a practical use. The two men formed the Edison & Swan Electric Light Company in 1883 to sell electric lamps. Their story of competition followed by cooperation was typical of the period. Many inventors were rushing to try to exploit the commercial potential of new technological breakthroughs.

## AS THEY SAW IT

❝ I went the other night to see the British Museum lit with the electric light, the superintendent of the Reading Room having offered me a ticket; it looked very well; and I also went last night to the Albert Hall ... where I found more electric light, but not so good as at the British Museum. ❞

—The novelist Samuel Butler writes to his sister about seeing electric lights in London, March 14, 1879.

# SHRINKING THE WORLD

**The late ninteenth century saw advances in communications and transportation that enabled information, people, and goods to travel farther and faster than ever. In communications, the telegraph was invented in 1837 by Samuel Morse to carry messages along wires. In 1876 Alexander Graham Bell transmitted speech along a wire and invented the telephone. The 1886 discovery of radio waves by Heinrich Hertz led to the development of the "wireless telegraph," or radio, by Guglielmo Marconi in 1895. Meanwhile, the invention of the internal combustion engine and the motor car revolutionized transportation.**

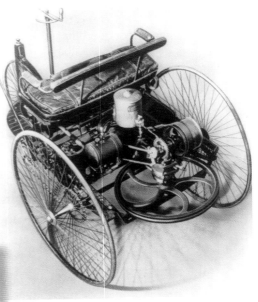

▶ *The first Benz automobile had a small engine behind the seat. Its maximum speed was about 10 miles per hour (16 kmh).*

## SOURCE EXPLORED

This map shows the international network of telegraph wires in 1871 (green) together with lines in the process of construction (red) and planned for the future (black). The invention of the telegraph in the 1830s was crucial in helping the US government develop states in the far West. It also helped Britain administer its global empire. By 1864, telegraph cables linked Britain to its vast colony in India. Two years later, in 1866, a submarine cable was laid across the floor of the Atlantic Ocean. This "thread across the sea" linked America with Britain. The trans-Pacific cables shown on the map were not built until 1902 and 1903.

## THE FIRST CARS

In 1879 the German engineer Carl Benz built his first gas engine. In 1886 he used this internal-combustion engine in the Benz Patent Motorwagen. The three-wheeled vehicle is now seen as the first automobile. After more developments, Benz designed the Velo in 1894. This vehicle had four wheels and two forward gears—it could not travel in reverse. Benz sold some 1,200 models. Within twenty years, motor cars would go into mass production thanks to advances in steel making and the use of the production line by US industrialist Henry Ford.

◀ By 1872 London was linked directly to Britain's colony in Australia, and by 1876 to New Zealand.

# TIMELINE

| 1712 | Thomas Newcomen designs an "atmospheric engine" that uses pressure from condensed steam to operate a rocking beam. |
|------|------|
| 1761 | *July 17:* The Bridgewater Canal, Britain's first artificial waterway, opens to connect coal mines with factories in Manchester. |
| 1764 | James Hargreaves invents the spinning jenny, which greatly increases the speed at which cotton can be spun into thread. |
| 1769 | Richard Arkwright invents the water frame, another great advance in textile making. |
| 1772 | In a legal judgment known as "Somersett's Case," a British court rules that slavery is not upheld by British law. The case effectively makes slavery illegal in Britain, but not in its empire. |
| 1779 | Samuel Crompton combines the spinning jenny and the water frame to create the spinning mule. |
| 1781 | Richard Arkwright opens the world's first water-powered textile mill in Manchester. |
| 1794 | Eli Whitney applies for a patent for his cotton gin. |
| 1800 | *January 1:* Robert Owen takes over his father-in-law's textile mills at New Lanark, which he plans to turn into an ideal community. |
| 1804 | *February 21:* A locomotive designed by Richard Trevithick, carries a load along rails at an ironworks in south Wales. |
| 1807 | *March 25:* The slave trade—but not slavery itself—is abolished throughout the British Empire. |
| 1821 | George Stephenson builds the Stockton and Darlington railroad. Michael Faraday creates the first electric motor. |
| 1829 | Stephenson's locomotive Rocket wins trials to run on the new Liverpool and Manchester Railway. |
| 1830 | *September 15:* The politician William Huskisson is killed by a train at the opening of the Liverpool and Manchester Railway. |
| 1833 | The British government sets up a commission to investigate working conditions in Britain's factories. |
|      | *August 28:* After a long campaign led by William Wilberforce, who has died in July, slavery is abolished in the British Empire. |
|      | Isambard Kingdom Brunel begins building the Great Western Railway between London and Bristol. |

| 1838 | **January:** *Samuel B. Morse first demonstrates his telegraph system.* |
| | **April:** *Brunel's steamship* Great Western *makes its first crossing of the Atlantic in under sixteen days.* |
| 1839 | *The First Opium War begins when China attempts to limit British trade in China.* |
| 1848 | *Karl Marx and Friedrich Engels write* The Communist Manifesto, *promoting a workers' revolution to overthrow the industrialized system.* |
| 1854 | *British physician John Snow maps fatalities during a cholera outbreak in London and learns that the disease is spread by contaminated water from a public pump.* |
| 1854 | *Charles Dickens writes* Hard Times, *which criticizes the conditions in which industrial workers live.* |
| 1856 | *A Second Opium War begins. It ends in Chinese defeat and further concessions to the Western powers.* |
| 1857 | *Sepoys serving in Britain's Indian Army begin a widespread mutiny against British control.* |
| 1858 | *Brunel's* Great Eastern *makes its first voyage. It is the largest ship afloat.* |
| | *After suppressing the Indian Mutiny, the British crown takes over government of India from the East India Company, creating what becomes known as the British Raj.* |
| 1863 | *Charles Kingsley writes* The Water Babies *as part of a campaign to ban the use of children as chimney sweeps.* |
| 1869 | **May 10:** *The Central Pacific Railroad from California and the Union Pacific Railroad from Iowa are joined at Promontory Summit in Utah.* |
| 1875 | *The use of child chimney sweeps is banned.* |
| 1876 | *Alexander Graham Bell invents the telephone.* |
| 1879 | *Thomas Edison invents the first practical electric lightbulb. Carl Benz builds a gasoline engine.* |
| 1886 | *Carl Benz builds the world's first automobile.* |

# GLOSSARY

**anesthetics** Substances that cause insensitivity to pain.

**aqueducts** Bridges carrying waterways over gaps.

**bureaucracy** A system of government by appointed officials.

**colonies** Countries that are ruled by another country as part of an empire.

**cottage industries** Manufacturing carried out in people's homes.

**cuttings** Open channels dug through higher ground to allow passage for a railroad or other road.

**emancipation** The process of being set free from legal restrictions.

**embankments** Banks of earth built to carry a railroad or road over low ground.

**enlightened** Having a modern, well-informed point of view.

**exploiting** Making full use of resources such as labor or materials.

**furnaces** Enclosed structures where fires are used to heat water.

**ideology** A set of ideas that inspires a political view.

**incandescent** Giving off light as a result of being heated.

**industrialization** The large-scale introduction of manufacturing based on machines and factories.

**internal combustion engine** An engine that generates power by burning fuel within an enclosed space to create hot gases that move pistons.

**locomotive** A powered railroad vehicle used to pull a train.

**loom** An apparatus for weaving cloth from yarn or thread.

**mechanized** Describes a process carried out by machines.

**mutiny** An uprising of military personnel against their commanders.

**patent** A licence that recognizes an inventor's ownership of his or her idea.

**philosophy** A set of beliefs that form a basis for someone's behavior.

**plantation** A large agricultural estate for growing crops such as cotton.

**planter** The owner of a plantation.

**socialist** Someone who believes that industries should be owned and run by governments and not by individuals.

**social reform** An attempt to introduce gradual change to improve the lives of society's poorest members.

**spindles** Slender rods used to wind thread around as it is spun.

**steamship** A ship powered by steam engines that drive paddlewheels or propellers.

**tramway** A pair of rails that provide a route for a wheeled vehicle.

**vacuum** A space that is entirely empty, even of air.

**workhouses** Places where the poor received food and lodging in return for work.

**wrought iron** Iron that is softened by heat and beaten or rolled into shape.

**yarn** Thread such as cotton that has been spun from plant fibers.

## FURTHER INFORMATION

## Books

Allport, Allan. *The British Industrial Revolution*. Milestones in Modern World History. New York: Chelsea House Publishers, 2011.

Burgan, Michael. *The European Industrial Revolution*. Cornerstones of Freedom. New York: Scholastic, 2013.

Hicks, Peter. *Documenting the Industrial Revolution*. Documenting History. New York: Rosen Publishing Group, 2010.

Morris, Neil. *The Industrial Revolution*. History of the World. Chicago: Heinemann Library 2010.

Mullenbach, Cheryl. *The Industrial Revolution for Kids. The People and Inventions that Changed the World, with 21 activities*. Chicago: Chicago Review Press, 2014.

Orr, Tamra B. *The Steam Engine*. Inventions that Shaped the World. New York: Franklin Watts, 2005.

## Websites

**www.history.com/topics/industrial-revolution**
An overview of the Industrial Revolution from History.com, with links and videos.

**industrialrevolution.org.uk/facts/**
Facts from a UK site for kids about the Industrial Revolution.

**www.mylearning.org/everyday-life-in-the-industrial-revolution/p-2355/**
A page about the everyday life of people who worked in factories.

**www.bbc.co.uk/education/clips/z9fvr82**
A BBC video about the invention of the steam engine.

**Publisher's note to educators and parents:** Our editors have carefully reviewed these websites to ensure that they are suitable for students. Many websites change frequently, however, and we cannot guarantee that a site's future contents will continue to meet our high standards of quality and educational value. Be advised that students should be closely supervised whenever they access the Internet.

## INDEX